Copyrigth©2021 by Unathi Kolanisi

No part of this publication may be reproduced, stored in a retrieval system or transmitted in any form, or by any means, electronic, mechanical, photocopied, recorded or otherwise, without the written permission of the copyright owner.

ISBN: 979-8-745-00186-4

To order books contact the author on 0719075241 and on email ukolanisi@gmail.com

Barren NOT Cursed

Tears of a childless Woman

Breaking stigma of barrenness

Voice of the voiceless

DEDICATION

To my amazing husband Lubabalo Kolanisi. You are such a rare breed not even a single day I felt unsafe or neglected by you or abused emotionally instead you have been a beacon of hope for this marriage, you kept on being the voice of reasoning and understanding that God's ways are not our ways and we have to accept our fate if it means that we must not have children or adopt let it be so. Every day you kept on showering me with love and support and overcompensate at times to close the gap of not having children by spoiling me at every chance you get. Thank you for being a God fearing man, thank you for you your unconditional love as you always say " I am here for keeps my friend you are stuck with me till death do us apart"

To couples with no children, God is not God of mistake He is good no matter what life throws at us ,He knows best may you be healed and find hope and solace in Christ it works , that is what has kept us going for all these years in our marriage HOPE IN CHRIST. May you be healed! May you be delivered! May you find peace and free yourself from chains of considering yourself cursed for not having fruit of a womb.

ACKNOWLEDGEMENTS

To God the father, God the Son and God the Holy Spirit who saw it fit for us to be called His sons and daughters I do not take lightly grace to be saved and called His child regardless of my condition for I know all things work together for good to those who loves the Lord whom He has called according to his plan. Today my tears of pain are tears of hope to someone who is not so strong as I am, it can only be Him.

To our families thank you support and love you have given us and never put pressure on us or call us names especially my mother in law and sister in law whom I love so dearly who also love me back as their child not as a daughter in law.

To our friends especially Nikelo and Fani family thank you for being pillar of support, you are always there and willing to listen and offer prayer support and emotional support. You took it further and share your children with us, you have no idea what it means to us when you share every milestone and progress of your children and involve us in their lives. Thank you we appreciate you. We are no longer friends but have graduated into family. and to all spiritual family's that we have served and shared the journey of spiritual life your prayers do not go unnoticed for us we know you always pray with us and hope the best for us.

MY HUSBAND REMARKS

This is proud moment for me as I celebrate my wife, my life partner who took courage and refused to be victim of this situation but decided to encourage families by writing this book. The purpose of this book is to remove the stigma and shame from God's people and replace it with hope and restoration, hope you will enjoy the book and find healing. It shall end well, as we mark our 14 years in marriage my wife without witnessing a seed in a form of children added to our family, this has been an area in our marriage where the devil has been mocking us and testifying year after year that our marriage is not complete until there is physical evidence of fruit produced out of this marriage. We are waiting patiently for God's promises to be fulfilled in our marriage as we believe that there is nothing impossible with God. Like Abraham when he and his wife went through the same journey that we find ourselves travelling but God assured him that his son will inherit all his wealth but at that time there was no sign or chance of this becoming possible as Abraham and Sarah were old but God came through for them. The secret that has carried me and my wife especially my wife is to believe in God and never stop believing His promises. "But as for you, ye thought evil against me, but God meant it unto good, to bring to pass as it is this day to save much people alive". Genesis 50:20 KJV

Mr L Kolanisi (Husband)

FOREWORD

Reading this book of a professional, business woman, happily married that is used by God in many ways has open my eyes as well as a man. Under the circumstances you find yourself in but you still manage to exalt God, the creator of heaven and earth is always a way out in circumstances and situation where there seems to be no way. I believe God was waiting for this book for His promise to manifest. I am a man but my eyes are wide open thanks to this book Barren not cursed. This book will open the eyes of many not only here in Eastern Cape, South Africa but around the globe. There was a woman with an issue of blood, her case of sickness never had a name hence it is referred to as an "issue". She had been to different doctors and they could not attach any name to her sickness. She was sick or bleeding profusely for 12 years but guess what? she was not cursed which is a proof that no woman or human being can bleed for 12 months and live, thereafter she lived her purpose. This book proves that these women highlighted in this book they were barren not cursed. Their children made huge difference or contribution in the history of mankind and in proclaiming God's word.

To the author, your bouncing babies are on the way. Barren not cursed.

Pastor XA Nikelo

TABLE OF CONTENTS

1.	Introduction		5
2.	Chapter 1	Pain of bareness	9
3.	Chapter 2	Complete family, yet so incomplete according to society standards	20
4.	Chapter 3	Pray to take pain away	26
5.	Chapter 4	Don't lose hope, help is on the way	30
6.	Chapter 5	Your children won't be ordinary	35
7.	Chapter 6	Serve or work while waiting	38
8.	Chapter 7	Holding on to God while waiting for prayers to be answered	43
9.	Chapter 8	Bareness lead to encounter and Intimacy with God	47
10.	Chapter 9	Do not lose hope	49
11.	Chapter 10	Barrenness is not a curse	51
12.	Conclusion		55
13.	Bibliography		60

INTRODUCTION

Women are under a lot of pressure from society to be what society expects them to be, should a woman fail to meet the ideal expectations of society there are names and ill-treatment that women endure. This book is about to break stigma associated with bareness that women suffer be it in family gatherings, work, church and communities at large. They are invisible yet their barren status is so loud. Women and couples with no children are known by everyone but yet their pain goes unnoticed. African societies have find way to position women with no children and place them in certain category of silencing them and make them to be invisible.

The bible in book of Genesis chapter 1 verse 28 (KJV) states that God said "Be fruitful and multiply, fill the earth and subdue it" What happens now when a woman cannot fulfill this instruction of being fruitful? What happens now when womb of a woman fails her? What happens now when the seed of a man cannot sit in a woman's womb? Whose fault it? Who must carry the blame and shame? Childless women are failed by nature and failed by universe and suffer fate that is decided by their bodies not to conceive not them. Majority of women wishes to have children and it is their desire since the early age to be called " mom" , it is every woman's desire to have a replica of herself but what happens now when that is not happening?

This book looks at one of the taboo subjects that women face in society which is a matter of not having children while married. Most women are called by names and suffer in silence while they carry their own baggage of feeling like a failure already. In some families they are even called derogatory names that affect them emotional and their social status. Even during the traditional events you would hear from songs that are sang and cheering they have lyrics that has a stigma around women who are childless for example if there are traditional events like umgidi or ukungena kwenkwenkwe *(traditional event of a boy transition from being a boy to a man)* you will find group of local women will sing derogatory songs that insult women with no children songs like " umfazi ongazalanga makabeleke ilitye" (meaning woman with no child must carry a stone) or songs like "uyabhenquza umfazi ozale inkwenkwe" *(woman who gave birth to a boy is superior)* or umfazi ongazelanga makavale ngayo *(woman with no child must take her private part and close them)* all these songs are sang in good spirit celebrating women who gave birth and now graduating to another stage of being called *" izibazana"* (which is mother of a boy who just graduated from being a boy into man) all these songs are sang without taking into consideration feelings of women who are childless attending the event or even thinking twice about singing them thinking that maybe there is a woman who came to support the family during this time of jubilation who does not have a child. Stats shows that if there are ten women in a room one of them is childless or suffer endometriosis or any medical condition that is preventing her to conceive. At times you will find in our African communities women with no children called derogatory words like *Idlolo* in *Isixhosa* or *Inyumba* in *Isizulu* which is an insulting way of saying someone is barren, at times these words are said directly to her during the heated argument or are said behind her back. At times you will find people talking and saying " no the reason she does not have a child maybe she committed to many abortions or she ate her kids *(wabatya abantwana bake)*. In African societies you find that it is even difficult at times to even have a word or reprimand a child of a family member if you are barren they will say " *ukhohlakele akanimba kaloku akayazi inimba(* which means she never gave birth so she has no feeling of a woman towards children).

This book aim at helping women who are struggling to fall pregnant or unable to have children to know that they are not cursed and they must be able to love themselves first before anyone can love them. The aim of this book is to break limitations and stigma these women face every day from society. This book will highlight some few stories in the bible where women were unable to conceive and God came to their rescue. It aims at giving hope to all women who are struggling to fall pregnant and suffer humiliation and judgment. The purpose of this book is to give hope to these women to know that they are not alone there are many women who faces the same struggle and who are in the similar situation but they suffers in silence because this is a subject that is a taboo to talk about.

Chapter 1

PAIN OF BARRENNESS

I was born in rural areas of King Williams Town in 1983, I am told that I was the first grandchild that my parents welcomed and the challenges that surrounded my mother's pregnancy and issues she was dealing with during the time she was carrying me led to my aunt who is my father's younger sister to name me Unathi which means " God is with us" or Emmanuel because they didn't believe that I will survive and be born so my birth was a miracle on its own little did I know that same strength and conquering attitude that I had before I was even born in my mother's womb will carry on sustain me as an adult to fight bareness, life has a funny way of showing sense of humor. I fought to be born yet but fighting was not enough I had to fight to conceive my own child and face daily struggle of fighting every month to be pregnant. The same battle of a womb that I fought to get out of alive as a child will still be same battle of a womb that I will fight to carry my husband's seed, life is a cycle that cannot be escaped , if I could quote Solomon's words from the book of Ecclesiastes 1:9 " History merely repeats itself. It has all been done before. Nothing under the sun is truly new. Indeed everything is meaningless.

I was raised mostly by my grandparents, like any relationship dynamics and challenges that lead to separation, my parents divorced when I was four years old. We are two kids in their marriage me and my younger brother but we come from a very big family. We grew up in a household where cousins and all children of my grandparents were staying under the same roof. My Grandfather was an Evangelist of mainline churches and we used our home as church for the branch in our area. Every Sunday morning we would wake up and prepare for the church service. Families would come with their children to church so I grew up in an environment where family life revolves around children.

I remember the first time holding small baby in my hand was my aunt's first child year 1994. I use to take care of her and not leave her bedside making sure that she is well taken care off. I would make bottle for her and know the temperature while I was 10 years old, I could change her diaper and bath her as my aunt has taught me how to take care of her. In my life there was nothing beautiful than this little tiny thing in my hands, my aunt would jokingly scold at me at time as say "hey you that is not your talking doll put my child down you think this is your doll" I would laugh because really for me this tiny beautiful thing in my hands was so beautiful and it was difficult to put her down. Little did I know that life as an adult has other plans for my life. I never imagine that I would struggle to fall pregnant. I never imagine that I could spend my 13 years of marriage longing for that feeling of holding that small tiny beautiful thing in my hands.

It is every woman's dream that one day, they will have children of their own. From an early age young girls are shaped by society to have an urge to be mothers. When girls are playing they always play with dolls or teddy bears as their children. They would dress up their dolls and make clothes for them. When young girls transition from being girls to woman they are taught about motherhood. When time comes where by young women get blessed by wearing white gown or traditional wedding society automatically expect fruit of the womb after all the jubilation of their wedding, even speeches from guest always talk bout "we expect many children from you" . When years pass by and there's no fruit of the womb. Comments start to come from family members and peers. In laws start to wonder when are they getting their grandchild. Church people start to ask questions as well. Questions and judgment from church people arise "is there any unconfessed sin", "is God punishing them" is there anything they are doing wrong? Have they dealt with strongholds in their family linage? Is there no generational curses following them? All these questions find a way of breaking the person who is in the boat of barrenness.

All these questions and pressure affects these women in silence. Women who struggle to fall pregnant suffer embarrassment and pain alone. Those who are lucky with supportive and loving husbands they face all these questions together with their husbands. Those who are unlucky unfortunately they have to face this pain and humiliation alone. Every family gathering or functions question will arise how many kids you have, when answer is none you would here the judgment with disbelief from extended family members "no ,no what are you waiting for we want to have grandchildren" why are you depriving this man right to be a father. These words pierce like a dagger in this women's heart but she has to show a brave face and smile with a polite answer "no we are trying"

Questions arise from barren woman, "why me Lord, is there a sin that I have committed.

Questions arises am I supposed to have my own kids or adopt? Does God see that I'm not worthy of having my own child? Waiting is killing you. At times you feel judged even to comment on things involving children. You feel judged to even correct children around you and pain consume and eat you up alone. I will never forget the day when one of my own family members threw it in my face the pain of not having children. I remember there was a dispute in my family amongst cousins and I tried to intervene and one of the cousin uttered words that made me to take time to release and forgive her and said " uthule wena uyakuzala kudala naba abantwana bakho bekhala ebuhlanti isibeleko sakho sigcwele imbovane" *(which means keep quite you barren woman your womb is full of ants you do not give birth, your children are dead)* that shuttered me coming from my own blood when my in laws never used those word to me, I had to pray and release the anger and hate towards her I remember her child was admitted to hospital and Holy Spirit said check out how is the child and show sympathy and caring towards the child, this is a child of the same person who insulted me and said awful and painful words to me.

Some women feel the pain of neglect from their spouse and filling the void of being alone, I would suggest that you find solace and comfort in God the one who created your womb and who knows the reason for closing your womb. It is comforting to find intimacy with God as He is the only one who can give you peace. Remember God is the one who created you in His image and likeness and He says He is closer than a brother. Spend quality time with the owner of your womb, he will comfort you remember He said He is closer to the broken hearted.

At times pain makes you neglect what you have around you and not appreciate it. I remember every time I used to cry and my husband would comfort me and say "I married you for who you are not for children, if we receive them it's a blessing but if we don't it is not the end of the world, it is ok" those words are what made me to stop feeling sorry for myself and crying because I felt like I do not appreciate what God has blessed me with , which is a loving husband but I am focusing on what I do not have. Also I have learn to involve my husband in my feelings also I had to remember that he is also suffering but as a man he won't voice out his feelings because he tries to be strong for me as his wife.

This reminded me same story in the bible of Hannah and Elikanah who used to utter similar words to Hannah. I have realised that God always makes sure there is a provision for a barren woman but most of the time we do not see it we always longing for what we do not have.

1 Samuel 1(4-8) And whenever the time came for Elikanah to make an offering, he would give portions to Peninnah his wife and to all her sons

and daughters, but to Hannah he would give a double portion, for he loved Hannah, although the Lord had closed her womb. And her rival also provoked her servility to make her miserable because the Lord had closed her womb. So it was year by year when she went up to the house of the Lord, that she provoked her, therefore she wept and did not eat, Then Elkanah her husband said to her, " Hannah why do you weep? Why do you not eat? And why is your heart grieved? Am I not better to you than ten sons?

God will make sure that support system around you is more than ten sons but at times we do not appreciate that and focus on what we do not have. Hannah was receiving double portion blessings from her husband but still her heart was filled with pain. She didn't see that her husband is in her corner that's what we do we don't see people who are in our corner and supporting us and focus on pain. Hannah's eyes were focused on Pennina who was making her life miserable not her husband who was loving her. At times we focus on what makes us cry and not focus on what makes us happy and smile.

I was raised by grandparents from my father's side, I never knew my mother because they divorced when I was four years old and she left us under our grandparents care. I grew up longing to meet her and to see her as I had no picture of what she look like, I could hear people from my village saying that I look like her, I am her carbon copy. I had this void in my life that I am longing to meet my mother and no one knew where she was. Everything was fine as I was raised in a happy environment but I was longing to meet my mother. The pain of not having my mother became more evident when I experience my first periods on the 23rd March 1996, I still remember waking up not knowing what was happening to me as there was no one who prepared me emotionally and psychologically for the change and transition that was going to happen from being a young girl into woman. My grandmother was old school and there are issues that I could not discuss with her. I remember feeling guilty as I was approaching her telling her I just saw something unusually happening to me and she called me aside and gave me woman talk. Little did I know that that day was beginning of a day that will control my emotions, my entire livelihood will revolve around it. I never knew that that day will always be with me and I will resent it in my adulthood when I see my periods. I never knew that in my adulthood that there would be time where I would pray that I miss my periods. My wish to meet my mother grew and changed into resentment. I resented her for not being there when I needed her to prepare me for the journey that was ahead of me of womanhood. I remember all my teenage years I was not normal I would get sick every time I have periods and would experience unbearable pain and abnormal bleeding. I would sit in a bucket and blood will just come out at times I would hide this from my grandmother because I didn't know what was happening at times I would share with her and she would come up with homemade remedies to help me suggesting that I must sit in a hot water with onion and she would make sure I am staying warm after that. The way my sickness advanced it ended up being everyone's business at home because for three full days I would be sick and miss school at times. I remember this Sunday I was sick bleeding abnormal and my grandfather went to get a bottle from the traditional healer from our village for me to drink and I could not finish that herbal medicine I only drank one cup but there was no change. I remember one day they had to take me to Grey hospital because I was bleeding abnormal and could not get up blood was just coming out and I was given injection and painkillers. All my teenage years my cycle was not normal even at school friends knew my business at times I would be standing In assembly line during morning prayers and blood will just drop and my friends would take off their jerseys and cover me and take me home. When I got married only then when I struggle to fall pregnant I voiced out my resent towards my mother for not being there in my childhood, For a long time I blamed her for not having children because in my mind I taught that if she was there when I had my periods for the first time and during the time I was having abnormal bleedings and getting sick maybe as my mother she could have picked up that something was not normal with her child and try to get help for me an early age. I always taught that if she was there maybe I could have had children, I channel my anger and disappointments to the wrong person I just wanted someone to blame because being there was not going to make any difference I only realised that in my late twenties that being barren is not anyone's fault and no one can stop it or prevent it even if my mother was there , there was nothing she could have done differently when your fate is decided no one can change that but you learn to accept your fate. I had to release my anger of holding her in my hearth and forgive her and move on.

I remember as teenager I used to picture myself with children loving them and giving love of a mother that I never receive. I remember making a vow that I would never leave my kids I will always be there in every milestone of their lives little did I know that universe or live had other plans about my life it will deprive me that opportunity.

At times I would ask God why would you make me suffer so much in life, I grew up without a mother and I taught I would love my own children like no bodies business but barrens happen why what have I done to deserves this in life? And Holy Spirit with a small voice kept on saying barrens is not a curse wait and see at time I didn't understand and even now I am still waiting but now I am waiting with hope that God will bless my marriage with twins.

Pain of barren women.

No one will understand it if you were never in the same situation

Pain of a barren woman no one can take it away

Pain of barren woman no one can cover her shame

She endures pain every day she sees her periods.

She prays every month to miss her periods

She prays that every month to feel sick and visit doctors room and receive good news she's been waiting for.

Pain of a barren woman.

Chapter 2.

COMPLETE FAMILY, YET SO INCOMPLETE ACCORDING TO SOCIETY STANDARDS

At times childless couples might not be bothered by the fact that they do not have a child because they know what they face as couple maybe a medical condition that is beyond their control but you will find out that society or external forces will be the one who are panicking on their behalf. They will always find ways to point it out to you that "you have a lack in your marriage" they will find ways be it verbally or indirect actions of pointing out to you that you are incomplete as a family. I remember it was year 2017 we were celebrating our 10th anniversary and we made huge celebration because we never had a white wedding so we decided to celebrate the day with our families and close friends. We asked one of the female pastors to do cake cutting and speech , in her speech she couldn't help to go and highlight that " yes we see they are celebrating their 10th anniversary and everyone is saying all good words about their characters and their love for each other but this marriage is childless" she called both our parents and made scene of people that they must pray over us to conceive, yes maybe she had good intentions but the moment and timing was not right as she did that I had my heart racing and my anxiety trying to overtake me and ruin our special day but I felt my husband's hand squeezing my hand so hard as a sign of relax, take a deep breath and do not let this ruin our day. I never felt pain of being barren like that day she pointed out to us that " You have a lack no matter how happy you might look or portray to be"

Society will try to steal your joy, the incident that happened to us when we were celebrating our tenth anniversary showed us that it take peoples word to steal your joy as a couple and even when you hear people commenting or passing remarks "no its too long now there must be a little one" meanwhile these people do not know what you are going through they just want to still your joy and in their minds you cannot be happy and celebrate your tenth wedding anniversary while there's no fruit of the womb to show your mileage of marriage, they make you feel guilty for being happy.

Don't allow it. I remember meeting this woman in a church who didn't know me and her first question was how many kids do you have and I said none she responded " *hayi hayi uhlelele ntoni ixesha liyahamba"* which means (No, No what are you waiting for time is running out and biological clock is ticking) my heart sank I felt anxiety and tears coming but I managed to compose myself and responded " If I was God I was going to know *ndihlelele ntoni"* (which means If I was God I was going to know what I am waiting for) , I ran to the ladies room and cried and composed myself and came back with smile on my face, this got me thinking how many people are killed and judged from church only for not having children by people who do not know what they are going through. How many women are crushed in traditional events *(eziko)* by other women who do not know what they are going through. I have made a vow not to attended any events where I would have to be in a kitchen with other women because talks will be about children and their milestone and their process of giving birth and you have to sit there and mile while enduring the pain inside.

"Shout for joy, O barren one, she who has not given birth. Break forth into joyful shouting and rejoice, she who has not gone into labour with child! For the spiritual sons of the desolate one will be more numerous than the sons of the married woman," says the Lord. Isaiah 54:1 (AMP)

You don't have to wait for pregnancy to be happy. God created marriage before children. Children are the product of marriage they are not your marriage. While you wait for your turn to hold your child in your arms you are building up a testimony. Those who trust in the Lord will never be disgraced but they will mount high like eagles.

News of pregnant people will reach your ears don't let it steal your joy. Visible stomach of pregnant woman will always be in your path don't let it steel your joy. Find joy. Baby showers will be organized and you will be invited don't refuse if you have strength; find an excuse only if you don't feel like but be part of the society don't shy away. Find joy while you are waiting. I have chosen to be happy and find joy and embrace people's blessings. If you are not finding ways to be embrace peoples pregnancy, baby showers you will open door for bitterness and bitterness consume your energy and kills you slowly. Bitterness will not change the fact that there is someone who is pregnant. Baby showers will happen with or without you the best way is to embrace people's pregnancy for your sanity. I remember in my early years of being married we used to visit people during December holidays and someone would indirectly to make me feel the pain of not having children and I would brush that off and send message to close friends who are always on standby when I crack. You need to find a very close friend that you can open up freely about your feelings that would just allow you to cry when pain comes ad hug you and wipe your tears away.

The Bible says the joy of the Lord is my strength. While waiting for this precious gift continues to live your life and enjoy every moment. While waiting for this gift from God continue to embrace your body. Continue to enjoy freedom of focusing to yourself and the privilege that you have no one to take care of except yourself. Enjoy the moment of not waking up and prepare for school morning rush. Enjoy the moment of having to eat what you want at the time you want with no kids to prepare decent meals for. Enjoy the moment that you could supper with anything you want and enjoy the moment with your husband that you can travel and see the world anytime you want and not have to wait for school holidays. .

Rejoice for you are not a disgrace. Rejoice and spoil your self and loved ones in the process.

Find children's shelter or place where you could channel your love. Open your heart to all those who are not loved. Be the help to those who need your help, for the desolated woman now has more children than the woman who lives with her husband. Spread out your home and spare no expense.

The book of Job 3:7 says "let that night be childless. Let it have no joy. "let the shame of being barren be cursed not you, let the stigma not stick. Find joy while waiting for a miracle. Speak the praises of the Lord upon your life. Barren woman you are not alone, many are suffering in silence with you. Their silence speaks louder than the footsteps of horses. The shame is not yours but your maker, remover your shame and embrace your womanhood. Break the silence of sigma let it not stick to you, you are not bareness but it is a situation you find yourself in that is beyond your control.

Chapter 3

PRAY TO TAKE PAIN AWAY

As a woman, when you go to period it is your body's way of releasing tissues that it no longer needs. Every month your body prepares for pregnancy. The lining of your uterus gets thicker a preparation for nurturing a fertilized egg. An egg is released and is ready to be fertilized and settle in the lining of your uterus, Barren Woman take note of this, it is your body that is releasing the tissues and preparing and egg to be released and be ready to be fertilized. What now when your body is failing you? Why must you take blame and burden of your body failing you? It is your body failing you not that you are the failure as a woman. Do not allow society portray you as a failure. Pray that God takes the pain away.

This reminds of story of Hannah, the bible says she was greatly distressed, and she prayed to the Lord and wept in anguish. 1 SAMUEL 1:10 AMP Hannah faced torment and humiliation from her sister Peninah. Hannah was abused emotional by someone she shares a table with during the supper. Hannah was abused by someone who was supposed to have her back as they are from the same family. Many times barren women face humiliation from close people. They face abuse from the same people who suppose to protect and fight for them. Peninah's are there to bring you closer to God. Peninah's are there to bring you to your knees , channel your pain into something positive in your life. Find something that you are good at and do it with all your strength. Focus on your energy on things that bring value to you, Peninah's must make you to be the better version of yourself. Peninah's must be the reason why you have the zeal and desire to be on over achiever, there is always a silver lining find something that speaks to you and makes you happy and channel you pain to it.

Close your ears to all taunting, be silent and pray. Choose to hear nothing and make no reply. For God will answer for you. Bless are those who curse you pray for those who hurt you. Luke 6:28

Bible says weeping may endure for the night but joy comes in the morning. Delay doesn't not mean denied. God's timing is not our timing. A thousand years to Him is like a day, a day is like thousand years.

Peninah's will be there to mock you. Peninah's won't stop but pray to take pain away. Don't ever avenge yourself for the battle is not yours but it's the Lords.

You will hear news about young cousins who got pregnant who are still in high school and have no financial stability that pain pierce like sword separating the bone and marrow, Pray more.

You will hear news on radio and television about women who left their kids to be eaten by dogs. You will hear about foetus that was found somewhere Pray to take the pain away. News of abandoned babies will always be at your disposal pray for God to take the pain away and not question why Me.

Pain is triggered by news of friends or colleagues who gets pregnant for the second, third or fourth time instead of crying and developing jealousy Pray and rejoice, be happy for them for every good gift comes from the Lord. Abraham waited patiently, and he receives what God had promised.

This is my daily prayer, that Lord take every pain away from every barren woman. Let them sing a new song. Remove the shame and stigma associated with barrens. Lord make the waiting to be easy and process to be painless. Close every void and loneliness. Comfort all women who suffer barrenness.

Chapter 4

DON'T LOSE HOPE, HELP IS ON THE WAY

Even in 2021 as African Countries we still have Peninah's who are bullies and bully Hannah's of our time. Peninah's hide their insecurities by being bullies and channel their energy into tormenting someone who is vulnerable than them. Tears of Hannah's make them to feel good about themselves. When Peninah laughed at Hannah's condition she didn't know better, jealousy overtook her reasoning as woman but Hannah did not fight her battle by being rude to Peninnah instead she fought her battle in her knees, she knew and understood that power of prayer changes situation. Do not lose hope, help is on the way. God hears prayers if He managed to open Hannah's womb what can stop Him to open our wombs as barren women of 21st century.

God's promise gives hope. God promised Abraham that I will certainly bless you, and I will multiply your descendants beyond number. Hebrews 6:13-14. Abraham waited patiently and received what God has promised.

I am writing this with tears as I have waited for thirteen full years to have children, I recently turned 37 years biologically the clock has ticked but I have chosen to not lose hope and put my trust in God, I strongly believe that God will make a way be it adoption or my own fruit of the womb. Stories of women who had their children over forty years give me hope.

As a strong believer and person who is rooted in Christ at times I faced judgment of not following the traditional ways to solve my bareness, I remember a family member approach us as said in a Xhosa culture a woman when she struggle to fall pregnant she is sent back home and her family must perform some rituals for her, we had to take a painful stand on this with my husband on this and declined to perform the ritual because we are both strong believers and we believe that if its Gods will for us not to have children let it be, this came with judgment that we have to live with that in your stubborn faith nothing has happen and we have to live with that and trust the Lord.

I remember even colleagues would suggest that there are traditional healers or someone who is gifted who has helped many people who struggle to conceive with his bottles and they conceived but we had to politely decline. Judgment will come that makes you even doubt your faith in God at times but still remember what God has said, and remember incidents in the bible that nothing is impossible with God.

Recently there was twitter trend where a man made fun of forty year old women who play with their two years olds and women who gives birth very late in life, out of this trend stories of women who had their children at the age of forty and over gave me hope, they are happy and filled with joy and with their two years olds, out of that trend I saw how society makes fun of women who have no children some don't even know the reason why those women are childless but society generally is very judgmental when it comes to women with no children they do spare their feelings. You could hear or see on social networks comments from other women that "I am turning thirty five and do not see myself changing diapers"

Abraham received blessings and promises before he had an heir. Gather your wealth and work hard while you are waiting for your child. Don't lose hope. Help is on the way. Hope is a strong and trustworthy anchor for our souls. It leads us through the curtain into God's inner sanctuary. Hebrews 6:19

And this hope will not lead to disappointment. For we know how dearly God loves us, because he had given us Holy Spirit to fill our hearts with his love. Romans 5:5 NLT

Then they said to him, "Where is Sarah your wife?" And he said, "There, in the tent." He said, "I will surely return to you at this time next year; and behold, Sarah your wife will have a son." And Sarah was listening at the tent door, which was behind him. Now Abraham and Sarah were old, well advanced in years; she was past the age of childbearing. So Sarah laughed to herself when she heard the Lord's words, saying, "After I have become old, shall I have pleasure and delight, my Lord (husband) being also old?" And the Lord asked Abraham, "Why did Sarah laugh to herself, saying, 'Shall I really give birth to a child when I am so old?' Genesis 18:9-13 (AMP)

Sarah was way passed her biological clock and she could not believe that she could conceive, it is like that even in us women who struggle to fall pregnant, you look at the biological clock and lose hope. You look at your age mates and feel embarrassed that at your age you will be running around with toddlers, question should arise whose life is it? Who are you living for? Are y living to please people or are you living your life as God has chosen to bless you with your life the way it is? At times talks and comments made by people shape our feelings and you also start to see they perspective that no thirty five or forty year old should be running around changing diapers of 2 year olds. This will need constant reminder the reason why are you still hoping for having a child at your age if you have passed the child bearing age.

Eventually Sarah got pregnant and they received their promised son, I sure she also suffered humiliation and shame look at the reason she took of making her husband to sleep with her maid servant Hagar, I'm sure she was feeling pressure and judgment from society and she ended up putting her marriage in risk just to please people .

I always pray that Lord you know the hopes of the helpless, surely you will hear their cries and comfort them. Psalm 10:17

Lord I pray for healing emotionally and physically for all women who feel under pressure and want to give in like Sarah. Lord I pray that you my close they ears from all outside noise.

Lord I pray according to Isaiah 53:4 that states that Jesus borne our grief's and He has carried our sorrows and pains.

Chapter 5

YOUR CHILDREN WONT BE ORDINARY

In most cases children who took long time to come are not ordinary children. We have seen many examples in the bible where barrens proved that it is not a curse, in fact the whole bible has stories that proves that barrens is not a curse but we have been shaped to believe that if you are barren you are cursed by God or punished by ancestors. Many will come up with their suggestions some will be offensive some will be coming from a good heart. I have experience may people asking me why not go for operation? Why not go for IVF, why not go to Mr " so and so" he is good with traditional medicine all these suggestions comes without being asked how you feel about problem you are facing it's a taboo question to ask or show any sympathy but they come from a judgemental point of view. I remember a high school friend of mine responding to my status that "they were talking with other former school mates asking themselves if am I not bothered by the fact that I have I no children" this got me thinking that our society has made this topic to a be a taboo people are not comfortable to communicate freely with people who suffered this fate and offer their comfort and shoulder to cry on freely.

We have different beliefs , some believe in traditional methods but to assume that thy have not try that is to insensitive, some believe in Western medical methods to assume that they have not try that its insulting the couples intelligence, some believe in Gods intervention and they know if nothing happened maybe it was the will the God.

Isaac pleaded with the Lord on behalf of his wife, because she was unable to have children. The Lord answered Isaac's prayer, and Rebekah became pregnant with twins. Genesis 25:21 NLT. This shows that it is God who closes the womb for His purpose. Today we are reading about twelve tribes of Israel who are the grandchildren of a woman who was barren

Out of Rebekah's womb came Esau and Jacob. Jacob became the line for the 12 tribes of Israel. Sons of Jacob are the foundation of the tribe of Israel. Grandchildren of a barren woman became the great nation. Fruit of the womb of a barren woman is not an ordinary fruit. Women who suffer bareness have great assignment to achieve. Find your assignment in the mist of your barrenness.

If we remember the story of Samson who became a judge, his mother was barren and fruit of a womb of woman who was barren became judge. (Judg. 13:7) and the prophet Samuel (1 Sam. 1:11), both of whom were consecrated from birth.

Also John the Baptist who was filled with the Holy Spirit his parents were barren but God blessed him from his mother's womb to be filled with His spirit and prepare the way for Jesus Christ. John became a powerful prophet.

In fact, he has a special role to play in God's plan of the ages. He will fulfill the prophecy,

Fruit of the womb of a barren woman always prove to the special breed. God always used barren women to fulfill His mandate.

CHAPTER 6

SERVE OR WORK WHILE WAITING

While you wait, serve God or find an organization where you can offer your love and services too like children's home. I always find humor in everything and use the old cliché of "if life gives you lemon make lemonade out of them", I believe in working in community projects funny enough before I even realized that I had a problem of barrenness I was looking for work and could not find work and I decided to approach one of shelters in my area and offered my services and I enjoyed that a lot when I look back now I find myself laughing because I managed to offer love and care to children that needed love and care who are vulnerable that means that now as a barren womb it will come automatically to love and care for a child that I did not give birth to, it was a boys shelter and I was assisting these young boys wit home work after school. I am reminded of story of Zecharia and Elizabeth. He was working for the Lord. He was performing his duties as a priest. He never blamed God and felt sorry for himself but He was serving in the temple and serving people of Go while they are childless. They still believed to God and hold on to His word. It is important to serve while you wait and not be away from God. Angel appeared in the temple to Zacharias not outside the temple. If he was not serving he was bitter he could have missed his miracle. We see two things happening to him while he is serving. Firstly, He had an encounter with an Angel of the Lord and secondly he receives good news that they've been waiting for with his wife. I believe that God was also moved by his commitment and dedication to serve while he had a lack.

We need to serve God, while we wait for our miracle. Be part of the community and serve Gods people. Be part of a church and offer your service to the church while barren do not feel shy to work or feel sorry for yourself and leave life of shame and not be part of serving in the temple. Be part of the temple. Your miracle and encounter is in the temple

The bible says Zacharias and Elizabeth were blameless before God. There were was nothing wrong with them that can make people to believe that they were punished or cursed they were **BLAMELESS** yet **BARREN**

They were both righteous before God walking in all commandments and ordinances of the Lord BLAMLESS, but yet they had no child because Elizabeth was barren and they were both well advance in years this prove that they were so committed until their old age to God while childless.

Then the angel of the Lord appeared to him, standing on the right side of alter of incense, and when Zacharias saw him he was troubled and fear fell upon him but the angel said to him "do not be afraid Zacharias, for your prayers is heard and your wife Elizabeth will bear you son and you shall call his name John and you will have joy an gladness and many will rejoice at his birth(1:11-14)Luke

It was Gods idea to make them barren for the time has not come yet for John to be born at times our times are not like God's time. John came at a right time to announce the coming of Jesus Christ. They suffered years of bareness but eventual God has open Elizabeth's womb for the time was right , by giving them a child in their old age. This proves that a day to God is like thousand years, thousand years is a like a day.

Barren women or barren couple were the parents of a child who came to announce the coming of Jesus Christ. Imagine if they have given up on serving and say "there is no God" they could have missed out on their opportunity to be parents. This story alone has given me hope that while you are waiting serves in the house of the Lord and be dedicate. While you wait for your miracle serve. Be part of community projects. Give your love to people around you, by doing that you are serving the Lord.

Keep on doing good. Serve God. Be consistent in your serving God might show up in your situation. Zacharia was so faithful in his duties. Serve your community. Serve your family don't get weary of doing good.

Involve yourself in community projects that makes change or an impact in communities. You can indirectly adopt a family child that you could assist as well by making difference in someone's life. You could indirectly be avail when people need help and assist. Keep on doing good.

Once you shift your bitterness and focus on what is around you it is possible to serve while you wait, I chose to mentor young girls to be better versions of themselves. I am amazed by what God is doing because He would just send people to me to mentor and people to guide about life and these people they always say we see God in you and your love and I get comfort because I am doing a difference in someone's life. I remember the girl I mentored her mother passed away every mother's day she would send me a happy mothers message and she would say "you play a role of a mother to me I look up to you" and these words will give me fulfilment to know that I might not have my own children but there is a child that I am making a difference in her life. My friends would also say " our girl children are looking up to you and always wants to be like you" and these message makes me believe that indeed God is good because there is no reason why He would make young girls to admire me but He send Angels to close the void. Look around there is an angel waiting for your love waiting for you to nurture, you are not curse when you are barren and that does not mean you have nothing to offer because you have no children of your own.

CHAPTER 7

HOLDING ON TO GOD WHILE WAITING FOR PRAYERS TO BE ANSWERED

One of the painful experiences is to hold on to Gods promises, while waiting for your prayers to be answered. The longer the wait the bigger the breakthrough. It is the painful experience to live and quote the word of God into your situation and nothing happens. The more your faith strengthens the darker it becomes but that does not mean God is sleeping or forgotten about your situation. My wait has taught me patience I have proved that I do have patience I taught I didn't t have patience but to wait for fourteen years and still waiting but still say God is good is not a child's play. I could have given up my faith and opted for other methods but I believe that if God said it surely it shall come to pass and while waiting we have decided to follow the route of adoption with my husband.

I remember I tried to attend doctors but to no vial instead every time I would come with bad news that breaks me and makes me loose hope. I remember 2012 we were having a revival at church and the guest preacher who was from Ghana he said that there are fifteen people here with prophetic gift and when Holy spirit touched them please bring them to the front and I was the first one to be taken to him as he was about to lay hands on me he said " my God , does she have kids, and usher responded and said " no she doesn't it" he continued and said " I see a black hand blocking her womb for her not to conceive so that her husband may be frustrated and divorce her but God will bless you with twins, they will see that you serve a living God, he continued calling my husband's name remember this man of God was from Ghana he didn't know us and didn't even now how to pronounce our names correctly but God made him to call us by our names

Remember God knows your names and knows the number of your hair so it was not a surprise to us when the man of God called us by our names because we know that God does not hide things in his prophets. This man of God say God is going to bless you with twins hang in there and this man of God didn't know that in my room there was a prayer with twins names written on it and we are still holding on to God's promises because we know that He is not a man that He should lie. What He said he will do, he will surely do. Numerous prophets of God who did not know us kept on saying the same thing when they meet us that God is going to bless us with twins and this is the message that we are holding to because we know that God once deliver in His promise before in the bible and surely He will also deliver His promise for us.

A child is a gift from the Lord, no one demands a gift from a giver, it is the giver who see it fit that you deserve this gift and when must I give you the gift so is God, He is the giver of gift and He is the one who has the authority to open and close the womb. The giver can decide to give the gift or not to give. Every good and perfect gift comes from the Lord and those who trust Him will never be disgraced and those who trust in the Lord shall mount high eagles maybe reason why child is not coming there is a abandoned and left in a children's home that needs warm home and warm families to show especially in countries like South Africa where babies are abandon every day according and research done by Medical research council shows that each year approximately 18.5 million children are abandoned and 4.5 million of those children do not live with their parents. During lockdown alone showed spike in abandoned children and stats of Gauteng province alone showed that 118 new born babies were abandoned in public hospitals since the start of 2020. God works in mysterious ways maybe reason of not having children is to give love to some of those children by giving them warm home.

It is not easy to wait but holding on to God's promise is better than stressing and living life of misery. Coming from a Christian background and also as strong Christian has helped me to hold on into Gods promises even if I see biological clock ticking.

If there are incidents in the bible of many women who were barren but God managed to remember them , surely it can still happen to me and you there is no other way but t help and not give not give up and also serve God faithfully while you wait and be consistent in prayers, people will always talk and come with discouragements like Jobs wife when she said to Job " why don't you curse this God and die" even in this matter they will offer unsolicited advice and commands "why don't you try other methods but this depends on the individual decision to try other methods to conceive but they come with trauma and expensive cost that not everyone can afford, stick to what you believe in , if it is God stick to Him but stick to what you believe in and hold on to it.

CHAPTER 8

BARRENES LEADS TO ENCOUNTER AND INTIMACY WITH GOD

May be God want to have an intimate relationship with you while you are still barren,

Barrenness leads to encounter I remember the story of Samson birth, the mother had an encounter with an angel before he was born.

In those days a man named Manoah from the tribe of Dan lived in the town of Zorah. His wife was unable to become pregnant, and they had no children. The angel of the Lord appeared to Manoah's wife and said, "Even though you have been unable to have children, you will soon become pregnant and give birth to a son. Judges 13:2-☐3 ☐☐☐☐☐☐☐☐☐☐☐

Manoah's wife received a visitation from an angel of the Lord with good news.

Your barrenness attracts God's visitation, remember bible says he is close to the broken hearted. He sticks closer than a brother. God works well in situations where there's pain and show up. Your barrenness might lead to an encounter. Your tears will cause God to look down in your direction and protect you and give you comfort in the mist of outside noise.

Judges13:8-9 and God listen to Manoah and the Angel of God came to the woman again as she was sitting in the field, but Manoah her husband was not with her. Manoah's wife had a privilege of seeing the angel of the Lord twice due to her barrenness. She experiences something that was not normal and never experienced by other women her age who are having children. God at times will make you feel special in your pain and makes you experience tings others never experience.

Manoah taught that they would die because they have seen the Lord little did he know that God was making them to feel special, God always works like that He will make your pain to be changed into an extra ordinary special story.

Today we read about Samson who was a child of barren woman, I'm sure in her pain Manoah's wife never imagine that she would give birth to a warrior that made exploits who killed lions with bare hands. Bareness leads to an encounter

CHAPTER 9

DON'T LOOSE HOPE

At times I feel like giving up but hope arise, I know there are moment when you feel like you are cursed, there are moment you feel like you are not woman enough but do not lose hope. When I lose hope I always remember story in the bible of a woman who was kind and built room for Elisha, this woman with her husband shows that they were good people who always wanted to help and feared God yet she was barren, they had no child but their hope did not deter.

Elisha said to Gehazi, "Tell her, 'We appreciate the kind concern you have shown us. What can we do for you? Can we put in a good word for you to the king or to the commander of the army?'" "No," she replied, "my family takes good care of me." Later Elisha asked Gehazi, "What can we do for her?" Gehazi replied, "She doesn't have a son, and her husband is an old man." "Call her back again," Elisha told him. When the woman returned, Elisha said to her as she stood in the doorway, "Next year at this time you will be holding a son in your arms!" "No, my Lord!" she cried. "O man of God, don't deceive me and get my hopes up like that." But sure enough, the woman soon became pregnant. And at that time the following year she had a son, just as Elisha had said. 2 Kings 4:13-17 NLT

Imagine we received prophecies as from 2012 but yet they haven't come to fulfilment that can make you to lose hope but the fact that three different man of God who never knew us came to us and said the same thing makes us to hold on to the promises of God and not lose hope.

Prophecies will come upon your life, God will send people to put you at easy about your situation. There are man and woman of God who are praying for you secretly. There are people that you are not aware of who are interceding on your behalf. Don't lose hope. Keep on showing kindness to people and they will make sure that they take your case to God. Who knows one day your miracle baby will be bouncing in your house.

Don't lose hope!

CHAPTER10

BARRENES IS NOT A CURSE

All stories that I have highlighted proves that BARRENESS IS NOT A CURSE, when I read these stories in the bible they gave me hope that all things work together for good to those who loves the lord. They showed me that God is the one who always control situations in our lives for His glory, am I pregnant? NO, Have I lost hope? No.

I want you as a woman who faces the same fate as me to enjoy your life while waiting, imagine if it happens that you die without a child that means you did not live your life to the fullest because you are feeling sorry for yourself. That means you are not living your life revolve around tis pain of barrens. I have chosen to be positive and enjoy the life that God has bless me with because barrenness is not a curse. People will talk behind your back and you will feel like you are not woman enough because of situation that you did not ask for, it is a choice to be miserable it is also a choice to be happy.

It is a choice to embrace life that God has bless you with and you did not ask not to have children, you did not chose not to have children but you can chose to be happy and learn to live around the situation or chose to be bitter about the situation.

We have made decision with my husband that when we are ready emotional we will adopt a child, there are other ways to be a mother. Adoption is another option while waiting for God to open your womb. We have told our selves that if it means let us love a child that was not given birth by us let it be so but one thing we won't do is to be miserable while God has blessed us with life we will enjoy life and serve God when He decide He will open the womb.

You are not cursed embrace your womanhood, maybe it is not meant to, be okay with that and live. Jesus proves that there will be people who are barren Luke 23: 28-31 He say fortunate indeed are the women who are childless. The wombs that have borne a child and the breast that never nursed.

Be happy, don't envy. Envy leads to bad taught and decisions. Envy leads to drastic decisions. Don't envy people with children be happy for them. When Rachel saw that she wasn't having any children for Jacob, she became jealous of her sister. She pleaded with Jacob, "Give me children, or I'll die!" Genesis 30:1 NLT

Because of pressure Sarah forced her husband to have a child with her maid. Don't be hasty to make decision because of pressure and jealousy.

When Mothers days are celebrated enjoy them with your husband don't let peoples gifts from their children make you jealous. Take yourself out or cook nice meal for your family and enjoy the day. Don't let mother's day drown you and make you feel less of a woman.

The painful period when schools re opens in January when people brag or celebrate their children's first days at school don't let it get to you. Social media can cause lot of pressure. Switch o off temporary during that period or just ignore the hype and enjoy yourself.

People will invite you to baby showers. Church members will organize baby showers, work will organize colleagues baby's showers don't let baby showers get to you. Excuse yourself if you are not strong mentally to attend them.

People will celebrate their children's birthdays. They post pictures of their children on social media don't let that makes you jealousy. Instead celebrate children of your friends and close people. Don't let birthdays get to you

Sing O barren woman, you who have not borne, break forth into singing and cry aloud, you who have not laboured with for more are the children of the desolated that children of the married woman, says the Lord. Isaiah 45:1

Which means rejoice don't feel sorry for yourself. Don't let pity consume you more than joy.

I want to break barrier and stigma in society and allow women and couples with no children to live without feeling shame and understand that they are not cursed. Society place limitations to people who don't have children. When they talk they assume that everyone has a child. In a room of 100 ladies chances are 2% of those ladies don't have children. As a barren women or couple take it up to yourself to make sure that they understand that you don't have a child and you are unapologetic about it. Don't feel intimidated because you don't have child, by not having a child does make anyone less of a woman or less of a human being. You are unable to have children or currently not having children but definitely not cursed.

It is time we break the stereotype and self-pity of women who do not have their own have children.

You are not cursed. You are not disadvantaged you are a woman in your own right.

The challenges of your life are no different from what others experience.

Being Barren is not curse.

CONCLUSION

This book comes from a pain of a woman who's been married for fourteen years without a child but having a support system of my husband and in-laws who are supportive make things very easy to cope with shame and humiliation of external environment, My bubbly character and personality also makes things easy on how to cope emotionally and mentally but I always feel sorry and place myself in shoes of women who do not have support system, who are abused verbally by their husbands and in law. I always think about fear and anxiety happens to women who do not have thick skin to take punches thrown at them by society who end up suffer server depression and others they end up divorcing due to issue of not being able to give birth. Other women suffer infidelity in their marriages where a husband chose to go out and impregnate a woman who will come and taunt the wife for being unable to carry a child and enjoy life at the expense of a woman who is failed by nature

This is a cry of all women who suffer in silence and end up feeling unworthy and invaluable only because their bodies are failing them to fulfill the word of "be fruitful and multiply" this book aim at breaking stigma of childless couples in African societies and allow them to adopt without judgment of being perceived as failures or support their choice if they chose to stay without a child if they are not comfortable with adoption. Tears of a barren woman goes unnoticed they suffer in silence yet their shame is so loud to the society. Let's break stigma associated with barrenness and show love and support to childless couples they also form part of our society even if they are not multiplying the population. Their voice is so loud crying in the wilderness waiting to be loved and protected. Husbands please shield and protect your wives from their in-laws. Woman you are not the state of barren and most definitely you are not cursed and you are not less of a woman by not giving birth. Walk with your head high and sing as the bible command you in the book of Isaiah 54:1 NLT that "sing, O childless woman, you who have never given birth, break into loud and joyful song, O Jerusalem, you who have never been in labor. For the desolated woman now has more children than woman who lives with her husband," I believe that God never cursed a womb of a woman and He has no intention to make anyone suffer shame and humiliation bible state that in Jeremiah 29:11-13 (NIV) For I know the plans I have for you , declares the Lord, plans to give you hope and a future ,then you will call on me and come and pray to me and I will listen to you, you will seek me an find me when you seek me with all your heart" God wants everyone to have great future and not suffer humiliation if your womb is failing you adopt a child and sing with joy as the bible said " you who have never given birth yet many are your children that means someone else is going to give birth on your behalf.

Barren not cursed

The only time God cursed a womb was when He said , a woman will give birth in pain , Genesis 3:16 NKJ " He said to the woman , I will multiply your sorrow and your conception, in pain you shall bring forth children" that was the only time God spoke harsh words concerning a womb of a woman.

God is the one who opens and closes the womb as He see it fit, remember the story of Leah and Rachel, Genesis 29: 31 NKJV "When the Lord saw that Leah was unloved, He opened her womb but Rachel was barren".

Genesis 30: 2 And Jacob's anger was aroused against Rachel and he said "Am I God who has withheld from you fruit of your womb? God is the only one who has a right to open and close a womb not mere human being.

Woman you have not failed, you are not a failure by not being able to conceive. God has the key who must be born or not born and at what time the child must be born or not born. Barren woman live and let go of anger and shame and let go of anxiety and live your life.

Genesis 30:22" then God remembered Rachel and God listened to her and open her womb" this proves without reasonable double keys of a woman to conceive are in Gods hand not man there only thing we need to do is to say " let your will be done Lord" and there is also no sin that you have committed by being barren remember Elizabeth and Zacharias in the book of Luke 1:5-6 NKJV " A certain priest named Zacharias of the division of Abijah, his wife was of daughter of Aaron and her name was Elizabeth was barren and they were both righteous before God, walking in all commandments and ordinances of the Lord blameless but yet they had no child because Elizabeth was barren and they were both well advanced in years." This couple was blameless and was coming from the generation of priest yet God closed Elizabeth's womb only because He can do so.

Sing childless woman

Sing barren woman

You have committed no sin

Society must sit up and take note of you and acknowledge your presence

You have a voice in society

Barrenness does not mean you are silenced or you must be silent

Speak up woman,

Let your presence be felt among other women

Do not shy away, you have committed no sin

Speak up barren woman, when they sing derogatory songs of childless women be the voice and ambassador for change,

Barren woman you did not ask for your womb not to carry fertilised egg nature chose to fail you.

Barren woman you did not ask for your tubes to be block.

Barren woman you did not ask for your ovaries to host and hub fibros,

Woman you did not ask to be barren fate decided otherwise,

Barren woman wipe your tears of pain and leap with joy for many are the children of desolated woman. Your tears of pain let them water your garden of hope.

POEMS OF A BARREN WOMAN

I. PAIN OF A BARREN WOMAN

Pain sharp like a razor pierce my soul
My soul why are you down casted
My soul is wandering and asking questions, what have I done?
What have I done to deserve such harsh punishment?
Is it a punishment or just unfortunate case?
Case that cannot be finalized for there is no trial to stand and present your case,
Oh yes a case, for she feels like a mental case when she cries uncontrollably missing a child she never met,
Razor cuts her confidence and kill her self-esteem,
Her confidence is destroyed by words of judgment,
Judgment throwed at her by people, who supposed to stand with her,
Her husband makes her a mockery by impregnating younger women, who can

give him an heir and humiliate her for not being a woman enough ,
She feels like a failure and ask question?
why Lord have you allowed my birth if I will suffer such humiliation of being a failure,
Failure at one thing that seems so easy yet so difficult for barren women,
Failure to multiply and replenish the earth
What have I done Lord?
What have I done Lord to deserve such humiliation?
Even birds laugh at her
Her pain is written in her eyes, as she covers her scars with make up
Scars that are created by the creator.
Who to blame when woman fails to fall pregnant,
Who to blame when nature fails to nurture her beauty.
Her beauty cannot cover her shame complete,
Her beauty cannot stop her tears from falling every month when nature fails her,

Her beauty will soon fade and there won't be any trace of her existence,
What have I done to deserve such fate?
Fate that is decided by my body without consulting me,
She chose to take matters to her hands and consult doctor's
Consultation that cost emotion and money,
Money that cannot replace the void of bareness
Every doctor's visit pierces like a sharp dagger piercing her soul,
Soul that wonder around asking,
What have I done to deserve such harsh fate?
Is it my father's sin or forefathers so that I can apologies and rectify their mistakes,
Who have I sin,
Sin that speak so loud for all to see and shame,
Shame that speaks louder than any voice,

Shame that shames her before she even justify your condition. Pain of a barren woman.

II. HOPE POEM

She finds hope knowing there's God who gives strength to the weary and increase the power of the weak,

In her weakness she knows that her strength is in God,

Her strength is like an oxen

Her eyes are fixed to the Lord,

Her hope comes from her knees,

Her tears of sorrow are not who she is,

Her tears of sorrow are not her destiny,

Her destiny is determined by her maker,

She knows those who trust in the Lord will mount high like an eagle,

She knows she has strength to run and not grow weary,

When external forces weigh her down she lifts her eyes up to the mountains and look for her help, no her help won't come from the mountains but her help will come from God the one who created her womb.

Hope is her

She is hope,

Hoping that she won't die without carrying her baby.

Hopping to be rescued by miracle of Sarah, yes It happen before why not me,

Hope to be like Hannah

Hope to be like Elizabeth,

Her hope is the only thing that can help her trough her darkest times.

She knows fear never builds the future, but hope does,

She knows when she chose hope anything is possible.

PRAYER

Dear heavenly father you are the one who know the number of our hair, you knew us before we were even formed in our mother's womb, Lord I pray that each and every woman and couple finding themselves in situation of bareness that you may give them hope and love. They must know that your desire is to bless everyone as you did not even spare your own Son, but delivered Him up for us all, how you shall not also give freely our hearths desire of a child. May we hold on to your promises knowing very well that all things work together for good to those who loves you.

About the author

Unathi Kolanisi is a born again believer and Minister of God's word who got saved at age of 20 years. She is married to Lubabalo Kolanisi they met an early age and got married who is working as an Engineer in a private company. She is married for14years without a child, For all their married life they've been hopping for God to blessed them with a child and still they are trusting Him, she felt compelled by Holy spirit to write this book when she witnessed and saw how barren women are treated by society. She felt the need to be the voice of the voiceless. She is a strong believer and minister of God's word and believes nothing happen by a chance. She has been through a lot of painful experiences in life but yet she hold on to her faith and trust God for she has witnessed and experienced the goodness of the Lord in several occasion which makes it easy for her not blame God for her bareness because she knows and believe that God never cursed a womb, the only time God spoke harshly concerning a womb is in the book of Genesis 3:16 " I will sharpen the pain of your pregnancy, and in pain you will give birth". Hence the title barren not cursed.

God never cursed a woman not to give birth but He delays the process. She believes in mentoring and impacting younger generation. She is a strong advocate of reality of God for she has experience a lot of growth spiritual concerning things of heaven hence she CAN NOT FIND IT IN HER TO BLAME GOD for her bareness.

She is a business woman who took a step of faith and left her permanent government job of more than ten years to pursue business. She started her own business called NATIS FOOD where she won title of being 2019 Engen Pitch and polish Regional winner and represented Easter Cape at Johannesburg which is a competition that set stage for entrepreneurs. She's also an owner of a micro franchise called MAID4U EASTERN CAPE which is a Recruitment Training and Placement agency for domestic workers. She believes in making a change and impact in her community. Both her and her husband serves in local church and has worked with many Pastors previously. They believe I Evangelism and winning SOULS FOR CHRST and deliverance.

She is a graduate from Nelson Mandela University in Public Management and currently pursuing her studies in final year Bachelor of Arts in Citizen Leadership and Politics majoring in Politics.

She believes that if life gives you lemons make lemonade out of them. This book will help many women who are scared to talk about their feelings and emotions. She wants to break stigma associated with bareness and makes sure every barren woman claim her voice back and shame the devil.

10th wedding anniversary 2007

10th wedding anniversary 2007

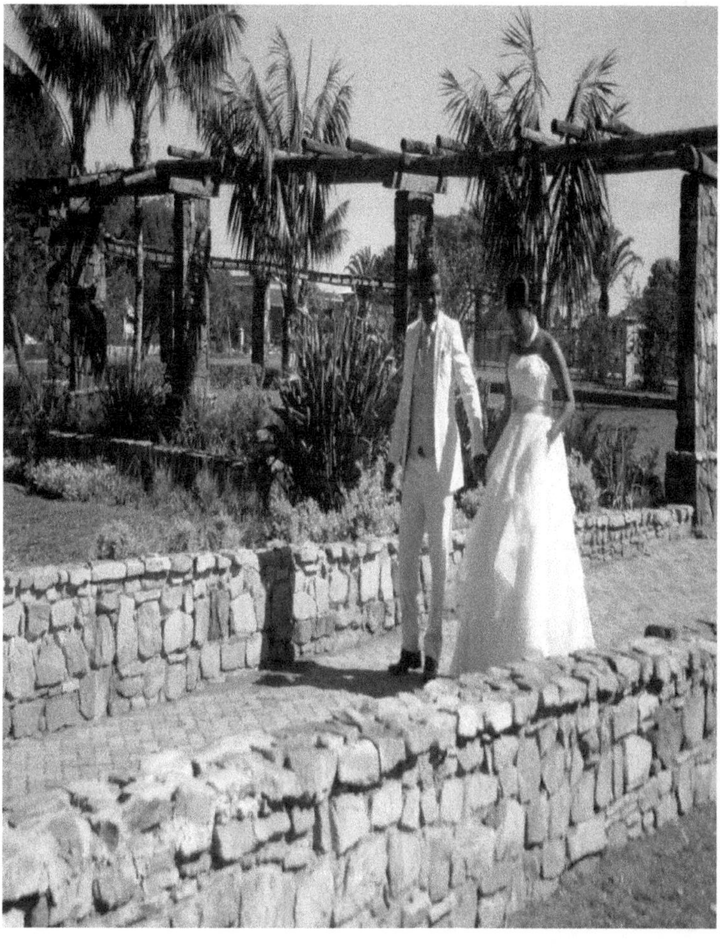

Having fun 2020

Horse riding, couple fun entertainment

2012 we are having fun in a Church event

Wedding guest speakers, we preach together. Couple that prays together stays together

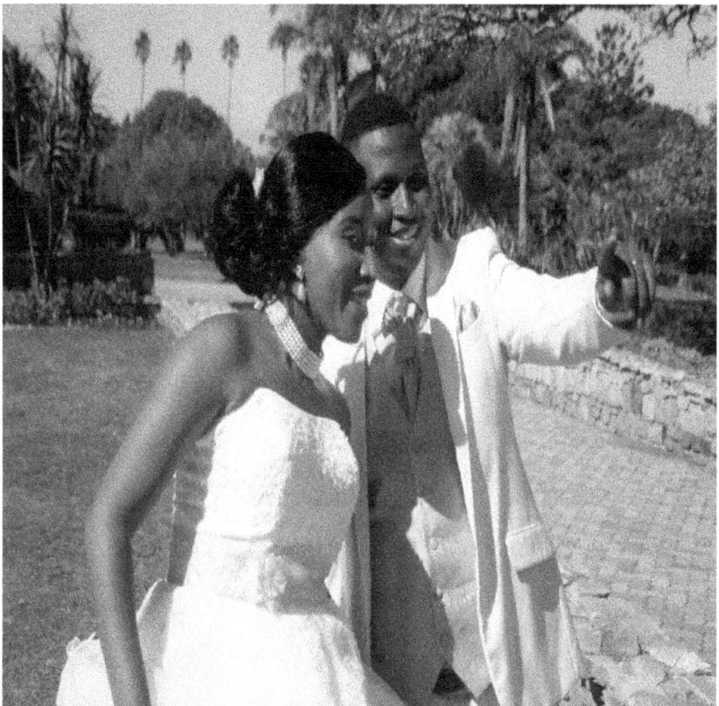

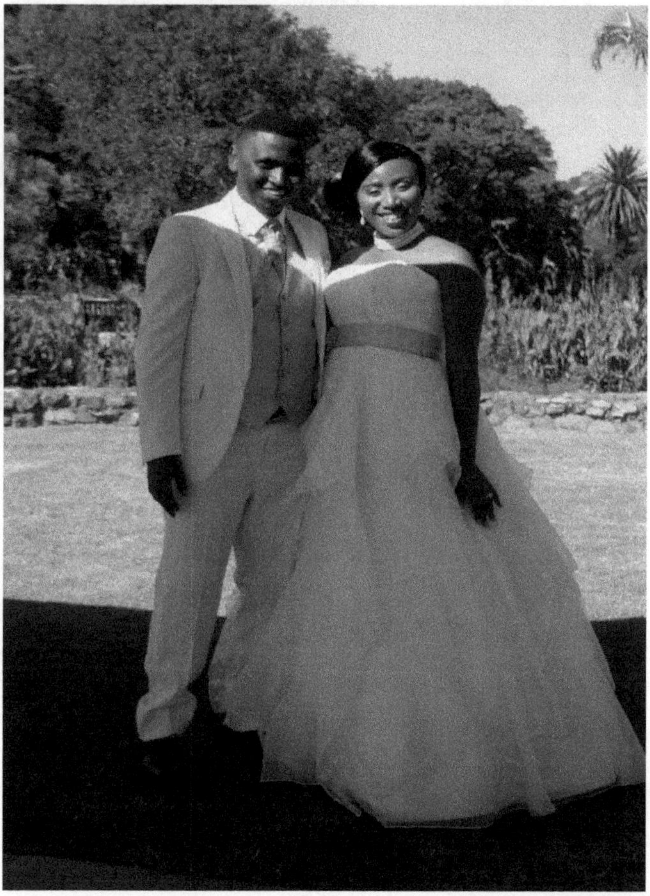

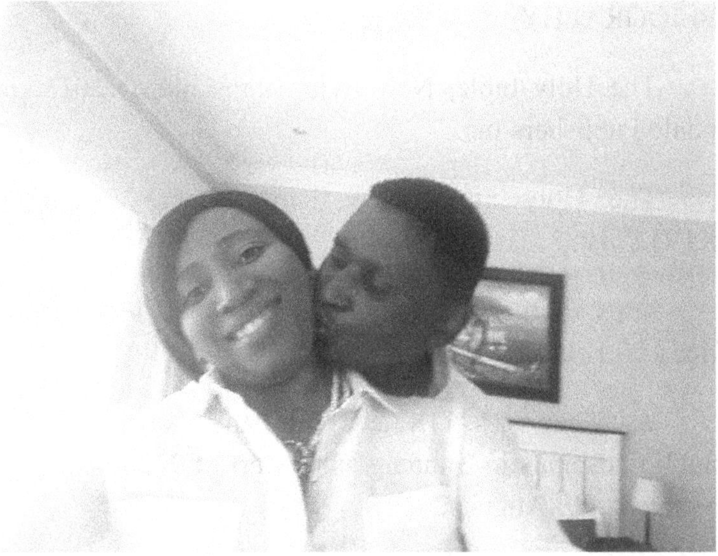

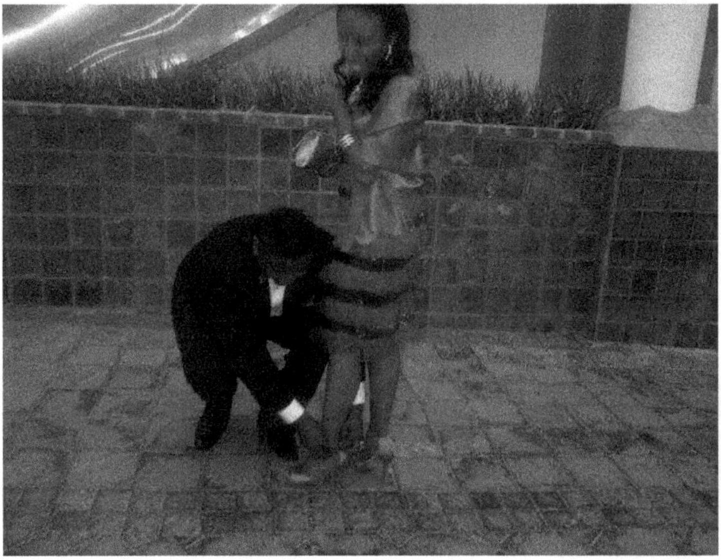

BIBLIOGRAPHY

1. The Holy bible, New living translation© 2015, Tyndale Publishers Inc.

2. The Holy bible, New King James Version (NKJV) © 1982, Thomas Nelson

3. https://borgenproject.org-aboden babies in South Africa (29 February 2020)

4. www.news 24 -118 new born babies' abandoned at public hospitals in Gauteng since start of 2020-health department. (13 August 2020)